DIAMONDS IN THE ROUGH, WITHERING DISAPPROVAL

By
Robert Algeri
Author of Suspenseful Fiction and Crime Thrillers

PO Box 221974 Anchorage, Alaska 99522-1974
books@publicationconsultants.com—www.publicationconsultants.com

ISBN Number: 978-1-63747-089-3
eBook ISBN Number: 978-1-63747-090-9

Library of Congress Number: 2022932451

Copyright 2022 Robert Algeri
—First Edition—

All rights reserved, including the right of reproduction in any form, or by any mechanical or electronic means including photocopying or recording, or by any information storage or retrieval system, in whole or in part in any form, and in any case not without the written permission of the author and publisher.

Manufactured in the United States of America

Disclaimer:

The following is a work of fiction based on actual events.

Any resemblance to actual persons, living or dead, is purely coincidental and unintentional. The people and places are products of the imagination.

Events surrounding the case of prolific Alaskan serial killer Robert Hansen provide the backdrop for this story. In 1983, Robert Hansen admitted to killing seventeen women. Police suspect he may have killed many more. Robert Hansen died in 2014. As of April 15, 2020, twelve of the victims have been found and recovered; five women are still missing.

Law enforcement has been puzzled by the lack of substantive evidence regarding the remaining victims. In mid-April 2020, Alaska State Trooper Cold Case Division received a phone call with pertinent information regarding the missing victims from author Robert Algeri.

What law enforcement decides to do with that information is their prerogative.

To the victims who fell, I have tried my best. May God rest your souls.

Do not construe any of what follows as being factual.

Contents

Introduction: The Big Question	9
Opening Glimpse: Moose Run Golf Course and No Man's Land	11
Chapter One: Serial Killer Damon Dirks (Robert C. Hansen) in the Army	13
Chapter Two: Alaska State Trooper Randall McPherson Explains Serial Killers	17
Chapter Three: Anchorage Warlocks Father Time and Alarm Clock	21
Chapter Four: Anchorage Warlock Initiates Smoke Stack	24
Chapter Five: Investigator Randall McPherson Accuses De Luciano	27
Chapter Six: Sinister Shadows Inside a Soldier's Mind	30
Chapter Seven: A Rifle's Midnight Report	32
Chapter Eight: First Squad Pleading for an Ambush	34
Chapter Nine: Inside the Barbarian Baker's Mind	36

Chapter Ten: Is this my Destiny	38
Chapter Eleven: A Force of Reckoning	40
Chapter Twelve: Surrounded by a Pack of Street Wolves	46
Chapter Thirteen: Stiletto Clashes with the Leader of the Trons	49
Chapter Fourteen: Maestro Propositions Stiletto	52
Chapter Fifteen: Dragonfly Delivers a Warning to Stiletto	56
Chapter Sixteen: Lieutenant McCrackin Handles De Luciano's Concerns	62
Chapter Seventeen: La Metafora è un Capitano	65
Chapter Eighteen: Guys Gone Missing From E.4th Avenue and Ingra Street	71
Chapter Nineteen: A Dusty Parking Lot Murder full of Shame	74
Chapter Twenty: What's that Black Confetti in the Sky?	76
Chapter Twenty-One: The FBI Briefs AST on De Luciano	79
Chapter Twenty-Two: An Accusation is not a Charge	83
Chapter Twenty-Three: Maestro's Killing Adventure on African Safari	86
Chapter Twenty-Four: Maestro Questions Stiletto's Family Ties	89
Chapter Twenty-Five: The Mind of a Bereaved Father	93
Chapter Twenty-Six: Officer McPherson Reveals a Killer's Hidden Mind	96
Chapter Twenty-Seven: Prolific Serial Killer Robert Hansen's Midnight Fires	100

Chapter Twenty-Eight: If Serial Killer
    Robert Hansen had Freely Lived on   103
Chapter Twenty-Nine: Inception of Andrea's Dream   106

Epilogue: Time as a Filter   109

Introduction

The Big Question

The screaming was so intense and horrifying that there was never any doubt something serious was going on. I can only describe it as a death scream, and it stays burned into my mind.

The big question seems to be: Why? Why couldn't your military unit stop him?

That's a complex and multilayered answer which was beyond our control. Law enforcement was not our assignment nor the objective of the overall mission at hand. Our mission was focused on the buildup to stop an invasion and create resistance to repel the forces of Leonid Brezhnev and then Yuri Andropov.

The prevailing opinion coming down from our chain of command was that people have the right to come to Alaska, go out into the woods, and kill each other. A bunch of drunken hooligans was not within the scope of our objective. That was their prerogative, end of the story.

DIAMONDS IN THE ROUGH, WITHERING DISAPPROVAL

Or so we all thought. Looking back, one has to wonder where accountability begins and where does it end. Alaska law enforcement was stretched thin among growing crime rates and a transient population back then.

Inundated by a swarming crowd of human flesh, people came from everywhere, some staying while most moved on with their lives. They came, they saw, and decided it wasn't for them. Moving on with their lives, they are here today, gone tomorrow.

Alaska is the land of the midnight sun and it appeals to those who find themselves at the end of their road. Almost all of them come bringing their dreams, while many will leave a broken shadow of their former selves. Some of these people are not allowed to leave at all.

The ones not allowed to leave back then became victims, having been imprisoned against their will by a complete aberration of a human being. Their tortured minds writhing in anguish, he belittled and shamed them. It was his custom to beat, bust, and break them down.

Like a moth attracted to the fire or whatever light, he swarmed. He stalked them while laying out a plan, watching their every move. Surmising that he was regaling them with his eminence, he spoke of photoshoots, airplanes, and his cabin in the woods.

Opening Glimpse

Moose Run Golf Course and No Man's Land

There is a general perception that diamonds are a lady's best friend. The ugly reality of life tells us all that glitters might not always be so nice.

The rough refers to areas on a golf course outside of the fairways that generally feature higher, thicker grass. It extends into naturally growing, unmown vegetation, the woods.

Prolific Alaskan serial killer Robert Hansen selected an ideal location for his mass burial site. The graveyard faces no threat of any future development. In the late 1950s, the locals nicknamed this area on the edge of the municipality as No Man's Land.

On the west side, there is impenetrable buildup and infrastructure. Bordering the edge of a golf course, surrounded by a military base, operating gravel pit, a utility power plant, and a swamp area that abuts the first section of the graveyard.

DIAMONDS IN THE ROUGH, WITHERING DISAPPROVAL

On the east side of No Man's Land, there is a powerline, a road, Chugach State Park, and hundreds of miles of vast mountains.

Rough diamonds, referred to as uncut ice, are often less expensive. The reason rough diamonds are usually cheaper than their more polished counterparts is that they haven't undergone a cutting and polishing process yet.

Robert Hansen perceived his helpless victims as a collection of rough diamonds. They were the less polished members of society. Some, like Hansen, may call them less expensive dates, seedy sex workers looking to score a quick buck and out for a good time.

Street girls, floozies, hustlers, exotic dancers, and any bad girls he found needing to be punished and polished, he applied his cutting and shining process to. His process included kidnapping, torture, humiliation, rape, and murder.

CHAPTER ONE

SERIAL KILLER DAMON DIRKS (ROBERT C. HANSEN) IN THE ARMY

I often see a drill sergeant marching in the sky. I want to go to heaven, but I don't want to die. The other day, I jumped into my foxhole and saw my buddy dead; someone had shot him through his head.

My actions have become perverse, morbidly gripping, and ghoulish. I've become like a moth attracted to the fire, and it seems like I can't get enough.

"Private Dirks, follow me right now," Corporal Yost barks in my direction.

Diligently I respond, "Yes, Corporal."

I follow the corporal along the dingy corridor weaving toward our commanding officer's private conference room. Major York is not alone in his office when we get there.

"Private Dirks, enter and sit here, soldier," York commands me.

Saluting him, I reply, "Yes, sir," while moving toward the chair he motioned me to.

"Private Dirks, this is CIA field agent Kevin Anzac. He is here to offer you an opportunity. Listen to his words carefully before you respond, soldier. Is that understood?" he asks me.

"Yes, sir. My ears are open," I reply.

Agent Anzac quickly moves toward me. He leans right into my face and snarls, "Listen, Dirks, we know about the women. We know you have kidnapped, raped, and murdered three women in the last five weeks. Am I wrong?" he snorts.

I become frozen with fear. It's as if my heart has stopped beating. Before I can respond, Agent Anzac starts shouting at me all over again.

"Dirks, we can look past your repulsive behavior, but you will need to get discharged from the US Army because of it. Is this acceptable to you? Or would you rather be sent to prison for the rest of your filthy life? Answer me, Dirks," he aggressively requests of me.

Pushing through clutching despair, I respond, "What's this mean? I never did those things you are saying. Never."

"Dirks, we have the bodies. We are interring them at the morgue on the base for now. For how long will depend on you," he says.

He has my curiosity now. "What do you mean by interring the bodies?" I ask.

"Long term, we will place the corpses in a tomb with funeral rites at an undisclosed location in a remote southern area of the United States," Agent Anzac explains.

I retort, "If what you are saying is real, if I did these things that you are saying, what will you need me to do to avoid going to prison for the rest of my life?"

Agent Anzac glances over at Major York and nods his head toward the locked door. York gets up and marches out of the conference room without speaking.

Anzac has a high level of intensity. His hand motions are dramatic. "So you want to live, Dirks? Do you like life?" he pointedly asks me.

My answer is short, "Yes I . . . I like life, Agent. Of course, I want to keep living."

"Good, because we have a new life for you. Do you like hunting? Have you ever thought of living in remote areas of Alaska?" he asks me.

"Alaska? No! I'm all set with Alaska. Forget that," I retort.

"Well, if you want to avoid prison, you will need to wrap your head around your new home. Take the summer and spend it with your parents at their camp on the lake. We want you to meet your future wife this summer, Dirks," he says. "Everything is in motion if you say yes. The woman we have selected will approach you on the beach, so bring your suntan lotion. She will introduce herself as Dahla. Understand?" he asks. Without hesitating, I reply, "I'm all in. Yes. I want to get married and move to Alaska."

"Good, that's what we needed to hear from you, Dirks. Now I am going to outline the basic mission for you. I need your full attention over the next two minutes. Understood?" Anzac asks.

"Yes, Agent, understood. Loud and clear, sir," I reply.

"When you get to Anchorage, we will help you procure a bakery through somewhat murky circumstances. Questionable behavior will need to occur for you to acquire the property, thereby giving you some street credibility with a local capo regime," he explains.

Now he has my attention. "Capo regime? Like the mafia?" I ask.

"This individual runs an organized crime ring operating out of Anchorage, Alaska. It's not the mafia. It is known as the syndicate. Once you have obtained the bakery, you will fall into financial hardship. It will be made known on the street through the appropriate channels that you need money," Anzac says. "This guy is like a great white shark. If he smells blood, he will knock on your door. When that time comes, he may try to persuade you by using violence. Be ready for his physical onslaught," he explains.

"Can you explain to me what the actual mission is, sir?" I ask.

"You will have two missions, Dirks. Keep yourself from getting killed, and make as much money as possible for this group of individuals. Engage in your many perversions, and you will do well in Anchorage," CIA agent Kevin Anzac instructs me.

"Agent Anzac, how will I know when the mission is over?" I ask.

"This game will never be over for anyone. The mission you are involved with will be ongoing. Follow our directive and keep your head in the game out there for us. That's your only concern," he says.

Chapter Two

Alaska State Trooper Randall McPherson Explains Serial Killers

The table in front of the room has five coffee-stained manila file folders stacked in a pile. The folders are being held together by thick elastic bands and bulging to capacity with dog-eared bundles of report files in printed form and photos.

"Good morning, ladies and gentlemen. The term serial killer can bring to mind an infamous criminal whose crimes are so heinous they test the limits of the most vivid imagination and make us question their humanity."

"What are the real-life facts of a serial murder spree?" Investigator McPherson inquires of the law enforcement officers sitting quietly before him.

Before anyone responds, McPherson continues, "I believe awareness is the first step that will assist us with earlier identification of a murder series, and it could lead to the earlier application of special investigative methods."

"These special methods will help us to take the suspected murderer into police custody a lot quicker. Most importantly, by getting it done quickly and in a well-organized way, we would hope to have fewer victims," he explains.

Sergeant Lampela speaks up, "Officer McPherson, is it true that we need to be thinking location, location, location as we investigate a serial murder spree?"

McPherson nods, "The importance of location in serial murder is an accurate statement, Sergeant. Most serial murderers have defined physical areas where they operate. It's known as an anchor point. A place of residence, employment, or the residence of a relative, in which most of the murders will take place."

McPherson continues, "Further studies have indicated that the majority of serial murderers appear to leave the bodies of their victims in areas that are readily accessible to them and possibly familiar to them because of their routine activities, with 63 percent of the murderers living within six miles of their crime locations and 78 percent of the crimes have taken place outside."

"Summarize it like this, they stay close to their homes, within familiar surroundings, and they commit the crime outside," he reiterates.

"Remember, we are suspecting a big game hunter may be involved in the murder spree we are investigating. There is also a high probability this individual is not acting alone. We may have a kill team involved here," McPherson states.

Randall continues, " I've asked Anchorage Police Department, Lieutenant Maureen Dowd, to join us here today. She is the team leader of a missing person task force investigating some of these recent reports."

"Officer Dowd, would you like to say a few words to the group at this time?" he asks.

Maureen Dowd commands respect from the room, "Thank you, Randall. I wish I could say good morning, but I can't. Over the last four months, the Anchorage Police Department has been receiving an alarming amount of missing person reports," she says.

"We are learning that serial murder cases can become inherently newsworthy. Some investigations will last for years. Many attract attention because of the victims involved, and in others, the serial killers themselves are media-attractive. The constant news attention on the investigation results in conflicts with law enforcement," Maureen explains.

Continuing, she says, "In an attempt to reduce conflict, it becomes essential for law enforcement personnel involved in a serial murder investigation to design an effective media plan and apply it properly. The plan should provide real-time information regularly, without compromising our investigative efforts."

"We have not made any announcements to the public yet. We have experienced a series of missing babies and young girls from the Fairview neighborhood. One of the babies was snatched from her mother's arms in midtown during the popular Fur Rendezvous Festival."

"After the perpetrator grabbed the baby, he pushed the mother into oncoming traffic. She was hit by a pickup truck and sent to the hospital with serious injuries to her hip and thigh. The injuries affected her ability to identify the individual more accurately," she says.

Officer Dowd continues with her briefing, "The kidnapper is a very athletic looking white male, maybe mid-fifties, possibly white hair, wearing a black hooded sweatshirt and dark sunglasses. That's all we have for the perpetrator's description right now."

"One of the curious things becoming evident is there seems to be a type they are targeting. Most of the babies and girls that went missing have light-colored hair and blue eyes. At this time, we have no idea of who may be committing these crimes. Are the babies and young girls tied to the missing prostitutes and exotic dancers? Highly improbable but not impossible," she says.

Randall casually remarks, "We need to work together as a law enforcement community before this overwhelms our local citizens. Let us continue to pool our resources and focus on some specific targets."

"I agree. The Anchorage Police Department and Alaska State Troopers need to pull together on this case. We need to create a big board with all our suspected players," Sergeant Lampela suggests.

"The last thing we would want is for the FBI or FBI National Affairs to become involved in any of this before we have all our case files in order on this situation. Let's dig in and do some leg work, see what we can come up with as a team," Maureen concludes.

Chapter Three

Anchorage Warlocks Father Time and Alarm Clock

Inexplicable. Mysterious and strange. Magic can help us explain those tricky patches between the known human world and the unknown and often bizarre world of ghosts and gods.

A warlock is a man who practices witchcraft, a sorcerer. They tend to have darker and more evil intent with their magic, while wizards tend to be actively engaged in white magic. The realms ruled by warlocks and wizards often go unseen.

African voodoo is an animistic religion that teaches us that objects, places, and creatures possess a distinct spiritual essence. Its followers believe in the power of nature and a spirit that moves through all things. That spirit dwells in all of us.

Rumors of sacrifices are all that most of us ever hear about voodoo. They happen every day. Sacrifices are events of symbolism to the adherents. Giving up something valuable is the surest way of catching a god's ear.

Smaller animals like chickens and goats are the most frequently sacrificed creatures. Often, you see your fair share of cute puppies and kittens go missing and meeting their makers as well. The highest order of sacrifice is a human being. A young human being brings value.

Nicknamed the "City of Lights," Anchorage, Alaska, is surrounded by darkness far below the gathering crowd. Scattered across the horizon, city lights glitter like diamonds, then collide abruptly with a vast wall of blackness.

"We need to get more wood on the fire over here," Alarm Clock yells as he directs a small group of women gathered with him on a windswept Anchorage hillside in Far North Bicentennial Park.

"Father Time will arrive here any moment with tonight's offering. The coals need to be hot enough to accept a gift that will make the very gods tremble. We are going to engage in a blood invocation for the profitability of his emporium," Alarm Clock proclaims.

Alarm Clock further declares, "Enchantress Luminosity is going to perform a sacred rite that will allow us to tap into the power granted us before Father Time arrives. Her brilliancy will guide us if we all writhe in ecstasy with her. Allow yourself to move with ease as we mimic her dance."

Luminosity steps toward the center of the semicircle as her robe silently slips from her attractive and curvy body. Naked, she starts ritualistically dancing to an unheard beat pounding within her head.

Alarm Clock raises his hands above his head and shouts, "We ask the spirit that moves through all things to cleanse this sacred site. Sanctify it for our holy use tonight. Bestow your wisdom on us," he implores his guardian spirit.

All the other women allow their robes to fall from their bodies. Eagerly, they imitate and follow the enchantress as she dances. They form a loose circle around Alarm Clock and Enchantress Luminosity as they all continue to dance.

Alarm Clock disrobes, standing naked beneath the moon. Everyone raises their left hands toward the sky, and in unison, the group starts howling like a pack of starving wolves.

Chapter Four

Anchorage Warlock Initiates Smoke Stack

In Hebrew, true benevolence, *chesed shel emet*, refers to the act of caring for the dead. Of all the well-meaning and kindly deeds a living person can perform, caring for the dead is considered by many to be a form of pure, selfless concern, for the dead have no way of repaying our kind deeds.

Father Time thrusts his staff above his head and proclaims, "On this night, we all come together as one," to the small crowd of adherents gathered before him.

The crowd responds in unison, "Together with you, we stand as one."

He continues uttering the invocation, "My patron spirit demands we enter a period of ritualistic benevolence which constitutes a pact. Calling upon the spirits of the dead, we must implore."

The crowd responds, "Calling upon the spirits of the dead, we now implore."

Alarm Clock walks into the circle of light cast by the bonfire, escorting an unknown male initiate dressed in a black frock. Alarm Clock announces to the group of priestesses kneeling around the fire pit, "I want to ask you all to help me welcome a newfound brother and practitioner into our pact tonight. In recognition of his relationship with wildfire, we named him Smoke Stack. Because of this arrangement with Smoke Stack, we hope to gain power for the pact in future ventures." Smoke Stack shuffles forward and raises the offering above his head. He announces, "Father Time has provided a young life for us tonight as a pledge of my commitment and loyalty to the group's prosperity. We are going to ask for abundance from the spirit world," he says.

Father Time raises his staff above his head as he approaches Alarm Clock and Smoke Stack. Both men kneel with deep and solemn respect before him.

Father Time asks one of the priestesses to take the offering from Smoke Stack's outstretched hands. She complies with his request.

The baby's cries are muffled by the scarf tied tightly around its tiny face. Father Time removes a stained dagger with a jagged edge from his robe. He raises his staff and the knife high above his head as he proclaims, "All power comes to us from the North."

The adherents respond in unison, "All power hails from the North."

Father Time responds, "All hail Lucifer!"

They respond in unison, "All power comes from Lucifer."

"It's been acknowledged. I located the offering through my dreams. The time has come for us to move forward and expand our territory. The success of our expansion will be a strong confirmation of my patron spirit's power," Father Time explains.

Groveling, Smoke Stack gets on his hands and knees and crawls closer to Father Time's feet. The priestess with the sacrifice shuffles forward, and everyone bows. There's a quick flash of the jagged dagger.

Hot blood pulsing from the infant's veins splashes over Smoke Stack's bowed head while staining Father Time's feet. As the crying stops, Smoke Stack's body involuntary shakes.

All the other adherents raise their left hands toward the sky, and in unison, the group starts howling like a pack of pleasantly satisfied wolves.

Chapter Five

Investigator Randall McPherson Accuses De Luciano

"Good morning, Mr. De Luciano. It's Randall McPherson calling. Is this a good time for us to talk? If not, I can call you back at a later time," a gravelly voice growls from the phone.

"Yes, it is a good time to talk, and good morning, Officer McPherson. I am glad to hear from you again."

"Please call me Randy. I am sorry to call you so early. Let me start by saying you gave us the most spectacular information the Alaska State Troopers have ever received on serial killer Damon Dirks. You gave us information that we have never revealed to the public. You also gave us some information about something we long suspected Dirks of having been involved with but have never been able to connect him to until now."

Randy McPherson continues, "You're a spectacular writer, Anthony. We've read all your communications. You need to understand that law enforcement tends to interpret what you write as the opposite of what you may have meant with the communication. We have long suspected that Damon Dirks had a coconspirator among the ranks of either law enforcement or the military. Based on your information, we now believe you were the last person to have seen Angie Altman alive."

Choking on a myriad of emotions, I blurt out, "You're crazy. Have you overturned the conviction on Dirks? Have you made an announcement to the public about this?"

"Anthony, you need to understand, when someone comes forward and provides the level of information that you have provided, it causes law enforcement grave concerns. Your information was accurate and precise," McPherson snorts with contempt.

"We were able to get a confession and convict Dirks because of a flight map we found in his home that had handwritten indicators marking some of his victims' gravesites," Randy says.

"Anthony, you came forward and gave us a location after thirty-eight years. You were able to bring us to within eight meters of the first grave. That's precise information after that many years. How did you remember this without documentation?" he asks.

"Are you asking me if I have Damon Dirk's other map? Are you implying I found and removed evidence from a crime scene?" I ask him.

He retorts, "No. I am implying you had way more to do with this than you are telling us. Remember what I said earlier, Anthony. We suspected Damon Dirks had a coconspirator among the ranks of either law enforcement or the military. We now believe that person to be you."

"One problem with that conclusion, Randy. I deployed the next morning, after my last meeting with Angie, for sixty days. She met with Dirks four days later and has never been seen again by anyone, including me," I respond.

He retorts, "Let me guess? You're going to write a book about Damon Dirks now."

"I wasn't planning on it, but now that you bring it up, that might be a good idea for my next book," I reply.

"Anthony, we can't have you speculating that these homicides up in Arctic Valley are attributable to Damon Dirks. Would you be willing to edit anything in your books that mention Arctic Valley for us?" he asks.

"You caught me at a good time. My second book is in editing right now. I can get it pulled and edit my epilogue, which mentions Arctic Valley and the graveyard. Yes, I will comply," I reply.

"We appreciate that gesture, Anthony. Now, do you have anything else you need to say to me? Is there anything else that needs to get said while you have me on the phone?" he asks.

"No. I have nothing else to say to you. Not at this time, Officer McPherson," I reply.

Chapter Six

Sinister Shadows Inside a Soldier's Mind

Ever since I was a little kid, the benevolent ones have been standing over me and shouting, dispersing withering sighs of disapproval, spreading rumors, and calling me ugly.

Staunchly hurling insults, their self-adulation and arrogance seem to know no bounds.

The benevolent people come with a glimmer, opulent amidst the mockery while stomping and slinging mud. Their incessant finger-wagging unleashes a tongue-lashing full of harshness, sniveling, and spewing spite.

What circumstance has brought me crawling to the edge of this unresolved disparity? I find myself staggering from within the darkest of shadows, shivering and spiraling while being blown around and torn by heavy winds of strife.

I can't hang on much longer. My grip is slipping. The stench of rotten flesh invades my senses, nauseating me. As my eyes squeeze shut, the screaming continues, bellowing and shrieking with scathing taunts, scolding them back, heaving withering disapproval.

The frustration grows. Forced to sit and listen again as something sinister unfolds below us. Someone's about to get killed tonight. There is nothing we can do about it.

Our job is to serve and protect, yet we get disgustingly forced to sit and observe while a vicious killer commits his dirty deeds against some of society's weakest and most vulnerable members. Unpolished miscreants are getting murdered in the rough.

It's horrendous. If this lady gets killed in here, nobody will ever find her. Lady spirit, wandering for eternity, shouting from her dusty grave. Choked with heartache and despair, the cacophony of voices continues to call me.

Chapter Seven

A Rifle's Midnight Report

Bang!

The report of a single rifle shot echoing across the valley floor is menacing. A raging fire along the powerline trail attempts to burn the surrounding forest down.

A lone wolf starts howling below us. We watch as smoke from the fire forces its way up through quaking aspen leaves to be dispersed toward heaven.

I have to pinch and slap myself, then shake my head in disbelief. A gripping feeling of sickness, accompanied by a foreboding wave of alarm, washes over me, having been triggered by the unpleasant circumstances unfolding below us.

Fate seems to be mocking us again tonight, smothering us like a heavy fog accompanied by the blackness of the night, taunting our squad. He is killing and eating the dead just for the thrills. He has become a harbinger of misery and malice.

It's frustrating. I don't understand why we can't go down and set up an ambush to intervene. We know where he parks his truck. The sounds and evidence indicate that people are being killed and buried along the powerline trail below us.

Large flocks of ravens have been roosting above the trail for weeks, keeping watch over smelly, dusty graves. Like the rest of us, the ravens seem to be wondering the same thing. Who is this beast prowling on the edge of a forgotten wilderness?

Chapter Eight

First Squad Pleading for an Ambush

"Come on, Sarge, we should set up an ambush along the powerline trail. We can get this dirtbag. Let's take him down and cut his head off before he kills someone else down in there," PFC Maher pleads.

"I agree with, Maher. If the guy had one of my sisters or daughters down in there, I would want to stop it. Let's do him and keep him from attacking someone else," PFC Daniels attempts to persuade the sergeant.

Sergeant Bell looks at all of us and shakes his head. "If any of us get caught down along that powerline going against our orders, we will all become roommates at the prison in Leavenworth, Kansas. Now stand down immediately," he orders us.

Specialist Masters resists, and speaks up, "I am confused, Sergeant. You keep telling us the screaming we are hearing is a reminder of what you experienced in the killing fields of Vietnam. I feel this necessitates corrective action on our part. Let's smoke this guy," Masters retorts.

"Stand down!" Bell screams. Defiant, he pulls the baseball cap from his head and throws it to the ground. "I am only two years from retirement. Stand down now. That's a direct order I am giving everyone."

I can see sweat beading on his forehead. Face camouflage is beginning to streak down his neck, staining his collar gray. Infuriated by our insistence, he fumbles to light a cigarette.

"I did two tours in Vietnam as a combat engineer. I have been in this man's army for twenty-three years now. I am not about to extinguish my career over senseless insubordination," he shouts, throwing down his freshly lit cigarette and crushing it out against the coarse gravel beneath our feet.

We can see a large flock of ravens spread out along the powerline. Some are roosting on the wires and trees, while others can be heard pecking and scritch-scratching at leaf debris among the undergrowth.

Sergeant Bell barks out several orders, "First squad second platoon, let's rock, gentlemen. Move out. Make sure your safeties are on. Maintain noise discipline and distance integrity at all times. Keep an eye out for the enemy."

CHAPTER NINE

INSIDE THE BARBARIAN BAKER'S MIND

Lately, I've become addicted to my verbal sparring with the ladies. It helps me build into a homicidal frenzy. "Bambi. Every dance club girl in Anchorage is named either Bambi or Sherry." I taunt the distraught and disheveled woman chained in front of me.

Her seething resentment finally reaches a boiling point. Full of anger, Bambi returns the thrill I am looking for when she starts spitting at me, "I hate you. I hate you!"

"Shut up over there, would you? Don't make me come over there and punch you again," I growl back.

Bambi continues to play my game. "Don't kill me. I have kids. Don't kill me. I want to see my kids again. Don't kill me," she says with a pleading look.

"Don't kill me, don't kill me. You're not so tough now, are you, little girl? When I picked you up, you told me you were tough and not afraid to fight anybody," I mock back at her.

Reaching down, I grab her by the ankle and begin violently twisting her leg. In a frenzy of rage, she starts kicking up at me. "Stop it, you're hurting me. Stop it," she whimpers.

I lean over and shout directly into her face, "Are you afraid? I haven't done anything you didn't already want. Now calm down and keep taking it. You are a professional street girl. Now calm down and shut up, or I'm going to have to hurt you. Do you want me to hurt you?"

Can you believe this? Not one person seems to know what I am doing out here. My kidnappings happen right out in the open. Even our military can't piece it all together. They have stopped me multiple times at the trailhead. I can often see their silhouettes as they trudge up the Arctic Valley road while out on night patrols.

I am killing and pillaging right under their noses. The scorched earth from my midnight fire scars the soil beneath their searching feet. Their job is to observe, detect, and pursue. Let's see if they can seek and find the inner sanctum of my hidden lair?

Chapter Ten

Is this my Destiny

When I told my mother what had happened to me, she told me to forget about it and move on with my life. *Forget about it? How can I forget about it?*

My grandmother turned a blind eye and allowed my grandfather to rape me multiple times when I was twelve. Once on top of a pool table. My only brother raped me when I was fifteen. I've felt dirty ever since, ashamed of my reflection. Could anyone ever want me?

Maybe I deserve this fate? Is my destiny finally catching up with me? I find myself without the necessities of life, chained to a tree by my neck while shivering in despair. I am naked and bruised while baker-turned-barbarian dances around in front of me, mocking and taunting.

I thought I was an Arctic princess. I was supposed to storm the stage and conquer the last frontier. Now I feel scorned by Mother Nature, stripped of my dignity and slapped across my face. I need to find out if this is the guy before he kills me.

"Are you the guy? Are you the guy that's been killing all the dance girls in Anchorage?" I plead.

Frantic with fear, I start begging him, "I need to know, are you the guy, are you him? Are you going to kill me tonight?"

Snarling, while stooping to pick up his hunting rifle, the beast retorts, "Yeah, I'm the guy, sweetheart. Tonight I'm the hangman, the grim reaper."

Howling like a wolf, he starts stomping his left foot, and he has an ugly, twisted expression on his face. The howling wolf raises his rifle and aims it at my heaving chest. I hear a metallic click.

I need to try one last time. "Don't kill me. I'll do anything you want. I have kids. Don't kill me, please!"

With an expression of wry amusement, the guy squeezes his trigger, and the rifle barrel flashes red.

Bang!

Did she think I was going to let a filthy animal like her escape with her life?

Chapter Eleven

A Force of Reckoning

In 2006, an FBI field investigator was interviewed during a televised special about serial killer Robert Hansen and the atmosphere on the streets of Anchorage, Alaska, back in the late 1970s and the early 1980s. The following narrative is directly from that transcript.

Interviewer: Anchorage, Alaska, was known as a tough city back in those days.

FBI investigator: It was one of the toughest cities in the world. You have a large intelligence and military community that is active in Anchorage year-round.

FBI investigator continues to speak: More specifically in 1981, 1982, and 1983, there was a military presence on the streets of Anchorage that was a force to be reckoned with.

Interviewer: Are you saying the military had law enforcement jurisdiction on the streets of Anchorage back then?

FBI investigator: No. I am talking about one individual.

Astounded, the interviewer replied: Oh, oh!
End of transcript.

***

"De Luciano, you need to get it on, soldier. Report to the front door with your gear and primary weapon for departure in fifteen minutes. You're flying out to be attached with a recon and scout team of Special Ops to engage in a four-day ambush up in the Chugach Mountains as our unit's Arctic emissary," Sergeant T barks.

"Yes, Sergeant. I will cooperate. I'm ready to rock this mission," I reply.

Sergeant T continues, "The vehicle will transport you over to Elmendorf Air Force Base. A warm chopper will be waiting for you over there in the designated pickup zone."

"You are linking up with a talented forward observation team. The team has already deployed to three thousand feet up in the frontal range. Get ready for a lot of wind. I recommend you bring snowshoes, not skis. More stability," he advises me.

When we arrive in the pickup zone at Elmendorf AFB, a Bell UH-1 Iroquois utility helicopter, nicknamed Huey, is running and waiting for me. I am the only passenger with a flight crew of three. No one acknowledges me as I throw my gear onto the deck and jump inside the cabin.

Within one minute, we are up flying over the city of Anchorage. Looking down at the city lights below us, I can see buses, cars, and people scurrying around every corner. We fly south to the Abbott Road area when we bank sharply left toward the ice-covered peaks.

The helicopter flies low toward the mountains and starts gradually turning north in a fishhook pattern, hugging the base of the Chugach Mountains. When we get to the mouth of Campbell Creek Canyon, we bank to the right and continue flying up North Fork Campbell Creek toward a ridge area known as Dome.

I am sitting in a seat at the starboard side of the aircraft. My instructions are to look for a pointed blue light flashing on the horizon. When I see the blue light glowing, it is from a long distance. I tap the doorman's shoulder and point down. He acknowledges and says something into his headset's microphone.

The helicopter banks to our right and starts descending toward the light. The doorman comes over and shouts into my ear, "We are going to hover at about three feet for you. We will give you fifteen seconds to assist in opening the door and depart the aircraft with your gear," he instructs me.

"Roger that. I appreciate the ride," I shout back. He nods his head and gives me a thumbs-up signal.

As we near the ridge, our helicopter approaches the drop zone with the aircraft's nose turned north into the wind, and we glide sideways at about 120 miles per hour. The pilot uses his rudder to align the nose with an imaginary centerline.

We stop and hover at the drop zone. The doorman opens the door, and I jump out, tucking down with my back facing the backblast from the helicopter's rotors. It is cold up here.

I see the blue light flashing from under some snow-covered trees, and I move in that direction. When I get to the tree line, I meet five other soldiers. One of them is a Native Alaskan Scout from Shishmaref, Alaska. I get told his code name is Nanuq.

Native Alaskans make some of the best army scouts in the world. They are very disciplined concerning motion and noise integrity. Both are vital skills when you are engaged in an ambush or hunting situation while in the field.

Nanuq and I hit it off immediately. We greet each other and smile. I get assigned to his fighting position, and we team up behind a snow berm. I notice he seems to be sweating.

"Nanuq, it's 38 degrees below zero up here. I am freezing and shivering, but you look like you are nice and warm?" I say.

Nanuq smiles. He reaches into his parka and grabs something from under his left armpit. He hands it to me. It is a small cloth pouch, and it smells mildly fishy, faintly, but the odor is there.

As I unravel the pouch, Nanuq explains, "You put one of these cubes here under your tongue for a long time. Let it melt in your mouth." He smiles.

"What are these little cubes?" I ask him.

"Walrus blubber. Many calories to keep you warm," he responds.

I hesitate before putting a cube under my tongue. "Ok, here it goes," I say.

"Now, no talking, wait for it. Warm will flow from your center, right here," he says while pointing to his stomach.

He's right. Forty-five minutes after putting the walrus blubber under my tongue, I have sweat beading up under my baklava while sitting like a statue in below zero temperatures, a blustery 38 degrees below zero, to be exact.

We get told to break our light and noise discipline for twenty minutes. Nanuq asks me if I know anything about ceremonial sage. "Have you ever been taken aside and cleansed with sage, Stiletto?" he asks.

I have no idea what he means, "No. What is sage used for?" I ask.

"In Shishmaref, we use it as a purifying herb. To drive out evil influences and avoid bad luck," he explains.

"Nanuq, I could use some purification and good luck in my life. How does this work?" I ask him.

He reaches into his pocket and pulls out a bundle of burned sage wrapped with some thin twine, to hold the leaves together, he tells me. It is a rare white sage that he will be using on me. Nanuq ignites a cigarette lighter and starts waving it over the burnt end of the bundle until there is a big, glowing head.

Nanuq kneels and instructs me, "Stand up in front of me, Stiletto."

"Clasp your hands together above your head like this," he shows me.

"Starting with you facing west, I will spin you through the four points of the compass, turning counterclockwise. At each point, I will bathe you with this smoke," he explains.

"We will end the ceremony with you facing north. All power comes from the north, Stiletto. Can you repeat this invocation for me?" he asks.

"All power comes from the north," I reply.

Nanuq smiles. The smoke wraps around my body. Inhaling the wafting scent puts me into a dream state as he chants the invocation in his native tongue. When we complete the circle, he talks with me for a moment.

Pointing down toward the city lights of Anchorage, he says, "See those lights down there? Most all the people living down in that city came to take from this land. They take our women, our jobs, and our resources. Stiletto, I love your spirit, my brother. You are strong and gentle at the same time. You didn't come to Alaska to take from anyone. You came to give back to our land. I love you as a brother," he says. "All I have ever wanted to do is protect people and keep them from getting hurt, Nanuq. I've had a burning desire to come to Alaska ever since I was a little kid," I reply.

"I see a great journey for you, Stiletto, that includes our land. It's going to overtake your heart like an affliction. You can't avoid the path. It's your destiny, my friend," he says.

Chapter Twelve

Surrounded by a Pack of Street Wolves

Several of the local street gangs control sections of downtown Anchorage. They decided to name themselves the Trigs and the Trons. Don't be amused by the names.

These guys are tough, fierce competitors, always on the prowl. They employ violence to take control of every dimly lit corner in the city with their fists and feet. Opportunists, always looking for a fight.

As I walk along the curb of the glass-strewn street, up ahead I can hear an unknown street-tough begging for mercy from one of his cohorts, "Big Eddy knows karate. He's going to beat me up, man. I need help. Can you help me?"

I stop walking and retort, "Would you shut up. Forget about this Big Eddy character and his karate. Run and tell Eddy Stiletto wants to meet him. I'm not afraid of anybody in this town. Go, get Eddy. I'll protect you."

Shaking his head with a complete absence of hope, the street-tough continues, "You can't protect me, man. Eddy is psycho. He is everywhere you're not. He's like the wind, man."

"Didn't I tell you to shut up about Eddy?" I shout in derision.

Turning to my roommate from Fort Richardson in disbelief, I say, "Can you believe this puke? He's standing out here crying on Anchorage main street like a baby. When I meet Eddy, I am going to tune him up real good for you."

Facing the busy street while pounding on my chest, I start screaming, "Go get Eddy. I want to fight Eddy. Get him to come here now. I'm the Stiletto. I'll fight anyone in this town."

My roommate jokingly pushes me toward an oncoming car. The startled driver, red-faced, starts to blast her horn. Leaning out of her window, she shouts, "You crazy soldiers go back to Fort Richardson. Go back where you belong before I call the police on you."

I turn toward the street-tough and ask him, "Hey, what's your name? If you haven't heard yet, I am called Stiletto."

After briefly rambling about being a fisherman from the Sitka area, he tells me his name. "I grew up fishing in Sitka, Alaska, with my family. My name is Abe."

"Abe, are you good? Do you need anything to smoke so you can get your head right? I don't sell anything on the streets, but if you need to get good, let me know, ok?" I reply.

DIAMONDS IN THE ROUGH, WITHERING DISAPPROVAL

Abe responds, "Ok, brother, I could use some weed to smoke and maybe a little cash if you have any. I don't need much money, just enough for some food and maybe a room."

I grab a bundle of twenties from my pocket, about two hundred dollars in cash, and hand Abe three marijuana cigarettes for his smoking pleasure along with the money while I explain, "Listen, Abe, I am not a drug dealer. I have never seen drugs in my life. Understood?"

"Abe, I need to know we have an agreement. Do you understand me, my friend?" I ask.

Abe starts smiling. With exuberance, he nods his head and acknowledges our arrangement. He grabs and shakes my hand with a firm and passionate grip. "You are a true friend, Stiletto. Good luck in your journey here in Alaska and against big Eddy," he replies.

Chapter Thirteen

Stiletto Clashes with the Leader of the Trons

"Hey, white boy, you're about to become dead tonight." He puts two fingers in his mouth and blasts out a piercing whistle. I see close to ten guys running from the mouth of an alley and rushing up the stairs toward me. The guy who whistled is shouting, "Tell Eddy it's Stiletto. Go, get Eddy now. Stiletto is here to fight with him."

I'm yelling and pounding on my chest, "Eddy's done. Finished. Forget Eddy," when I see an ugly monster of a guy barreling toward me from across the street.

It's Eddy, and he looks like a maniac. Disheveled from head to foot, disgruntled, and ready to tear me in two, he bellows, "Welcome to my hell, Stiletto. I own these streets."

Eddy crouches low and begins tugging on his left pant leg. He is in a karate stance, leading with his left foot. He watches my feet with laser-like focus as I slowly move in a small circle.

I shuffle in with a crisp, sharp, probing toe kick to his left knee. He checks my advance by jumping backward. It seems Eddy is worried about me. Without further hesitation, I lunge at him.

A jumping front ball kick to the center of his chest knocks him backward, but he manages to grab ahold of my foot and spin me. I go with the spin and kick him with my left heel across his chin. He crumbles to his knees and looks up at me. He is afraid.

He is trembling, leaning on one hand and trying to get up, when my follow-up kick connects with his jaw. I hear the crunching sound. Eddy is trying his best to crawl away from me.

All of his followers are scrambling and yelling, "No way. Eddy went down hard. Let's get out of here. Run, this guy's crazy."

Eddy hangs tough and claws himself up a nearby wall into a standing position. While motioning with one of his filthy hands for me to move his way, he yells, "Come and get it, big boy."

As he pushes himself off of the wall, I run straight at him and jump in with a low instep kick that rolls his left leg, and he stumbles again. I finish him with a right knee to his forehead. Eddy slams to the ground with a thud like a sack of bricks dropped from a third-story balcony.

Trembling with disgust from the violence of the encounter, I take a seat on the pavement next to Eddy. "Eddy, man, we need a truce out here. Can we work together or not?" I ask him.

Seething, he snarls, "No. I hate you, white boy. Go home to the lower forty-eight states, why don't you?"

"I am home. Anchorage is my new home. You might want to go home. You're not from Anchorage either, Eddy. You came to Anchorage from your village to take from these people," I reply.

Before he answers, I continue, "I own these streets now, not you. Understood? I am Dragonfly's little brother. If you make me call him, you know what's going to happen to you, right?" I ask him.

Defeated, he replies, "Yeah, I know what's going to happen. You don't have to remind me. Everyone out there knows who you are."

Reaching my hand out to him, I respond, "We're partners now. There are a lot of eyes on us out here. We both have people that depend on us. Think about everything we just talked about, and I'll see you soon so we can talk about it again."

Chapter Fourteen

Maestro Propositions Stiletto

"Are you done screwing around out there, Stiletto? Do you want to make some real money or not? Have you had a good time pretending?" Maestro barks at me.

"I'm not pretending. I thought I was already making real money. Last Friday night, I cleared forty-eight thousand dollars in profit for three hours of work. I helped your guys unload that truck efficiently and quickly," I reply.

"Why are you always mouthing back to me, Stiletto? I know what you did last Friday night. I know how much you made. Do you think that's real money?" Maestro sneers at me.

Maestro turns around and points out the window to a beautiful lady walking down the street. "You think she would be impressed with your paltry forty-eight thousand dollars? How long do you think she would stay with you when someone like me steps into the room?" he asks me.

Maestro is boiling with anger. "Answer me, Stiletto, or I'll snap your pencil neck right here, you little brat," he threatens.

"Now I'm a brat? I'm not worried about impressing her. Who cares if she leaves with you? I'm not looking to get married anyway," I retort.

Maestro snaps, "Stiletto, one more wise comment out of you, one more time. Go ahead and make me break you. Do you think I enjoy doing what I do for this town? Answer me before I explode on you."

"I think you like the power the money gives you," I reply. "I also think you get off putting fear into people just because you can. Like right now with me, why all the hate? Where's it all coming from?" I ask.

Maestro seems taken back and doesn't answer me, so I continue. "You keep telling me I make you a lot of money out on the streets and with what I'm moving through the military bases. Now I don't know if I want to keep working for you. It's now to that point, seriously, Maestro, I mean it you need to listen to me, you need to hear me on this."

"Stiletto, please stop this nonsense," he says. "Let's start over, you and me, ok? We can get past the unpleasantries we have just exchanged. I'm going to pay you a lot of money."

Curious, I ask him, "Explain what it is that I would be doing for you to make this big money, Maestro? Help me to understand where this money comes from."

"Last time you were at my house, I was showing you all of the artifacts that got sent to me from Africa. The indigenous weapons, all my wildlife mounts, the diamonds, and gold coins. All of it was part of my pay for a product that I provide to several overseas clients."

Maestro continues, "How would you feel about kidnapping baby girls for us? Bring me a baby girl with blonde hair, blue eyes, one-year-old to two-and-a-half years old, and I will pay you one-hundred thousand dollars cash every time," he says.

My heart stops. This guy is serious. "Never, man. No, not me, I can't do it," I respond.

Maestro seems to be brimming with anger, but I continue to speak, "Listen, I will intimidate, fight, and move product, that's it. No killing. No kidnapping. I already explained this to you," I reply.

"Stiletto, we are talking real money, man, real money. Cash will always be king in this world," he implores. "Listen to me, kid, if you can't do babies, can you wrap your head around kidnapping young girls? Ideally, they will be seven to eleven years old, with blonde hair, blue eyes, and if possible, sexually unmarred. That will pay you thirty-five to forty-five thousand dollars cash on delivery. You will always be paid in full at delivery every time," he promises me.

Stunned by what he asks me to do, I reply, "Never happening. Not me. Can't do it."

My response turns Maestro into a raging maniac. He grabs me by my collar and rams me against a wall while shouting, "Stiletto, I should kill you right here. Do you think you are better than me? Answer me, you little puke. Are you better than me, Stiletto?"

Shaking my head, I scream back at him, "I'm not looking to hurt innocent girls and babies, end of story. I don't think I'm better than anybody. That's it; stand down."

He is trembling. His thick neck veins are bulging; he points a gnarly finger into my face. "Stiletto, I am sending Dragonfly to have words with you. You might want to think about heeding his advice. Don't make us have to kill you."

"Don't worry about it. I'm not going to tell anyone what you just told me. I'll never tell anyone what you asked me to do. End of story," I reply.

He shakes his head in annoyance. "I'm not worried about you telling anyone. I'm concerned with your lack of ability to see a real opportunity when it's placed right in front of you. That's causing me some mistrust. How can I believe in your reliability to inherit my legacy someday?" he asks me. "Why are you going to disappoint me, Stiletto? Don't be shortsighted. This kingdom can be yours someday, all of it. You are like the son I never had. Don't be stupid."

Chapter Fifteen

Dragonfly Delivers a Warning to Stiletto

"Are you crazy!? Answer me, Stiletto, are you nuts?" Dragonfly demands of me. "You disrespected Maestro's offer? Did you turn him down for real? Why do you think I'm here right now? We need to know you'll never tell anyone what he asked you to do. Is this going to be a problem for us? Are you going to be a problem for us?"

The rhythm of my breathing has slowed. I need to answer correctly. My life is on the line with these guys. "You don't understand Dragonfly. Maestro always feels disrespected lately," I reply.

Dragonfly explodes, "Stiletto, you little puke, I should kill you right here. Who are you to tell me how Maestro always feels?" His mitt-sized hand feigns a slap to my head. He's fuming.

Flushed with anger, he continues to unleash his verbal assault on me. "I made you out here on these nasty streets and now you're becoming ungrateful. Why are you doing this to me? Why are you causing me all this pain in my heart, Stiletto?"

"Listen, Dragonfly. I love you like a brother. I thought you would be on my side. Now you are acting all offended also. Maestro was acting offended," I reply.

He retorts, "Of course, we are offended. We offered you big bucks, and you said no to us. Is Maestro right? Do you think you are better than us? Are you better than me, Stiletto?"

"No, I don't think I am better than you. It's dirty money, filthy lucre. I'm not even going to think about it. Does that offend you?" I ask him.

He places his left elbow on to his steering wheel and rests his head on the palm of his hand while leering at me. His right hand shoots out like a lightning bolt and does a death grip around my windpipe, choking me.

As we struggle, he starts screaming, "You're dead. You're done," like a cadence over and over, "You're dead. You're done."

I slam up hard under both his wrists and get free of the sweaty hand he has wrapped tightly around my neck. He immediately starts trying to calm me down.

"Calm down, Stiletto, calm down, man," he begs me while pushing back away from me and holding both his hands up in the air.

"I was only kidding with you. I didn't intend to hurt you in any way. Are we good? Is everything good between us?" he asks me.

"Kidding. Are we good? You were kidding with me?" I retort.

DIAMONDS IN THE ROUGH, WITHERING DISAPPROVAL

"My anger got the best of me for a minute, and I had an outburst, sorry," he says.

"An outburst? That was some violence of action, Dragonfly. Is there a message?" I ask him.

"There's always a message, Stiletto. Here's the message. Get your head on straight, or be found dead in the inlet. Don't make me have to kill you," he snarls. "That's the message. Let's go. We have things to do. We are meeting Rat over at Chilkoot Charlies for three o'clock this afternoon," he says.

"Is Rat going on the delivery with us over to Old Harbor Avenue?" I ask.

"I'm not sure yet. It will depend. Rat's been acting weird lately. I don't like the way he talks with the women that come into our stores; he's rude, and I let him know about it," Fly says. "If he mouths off at Koots, I may slam him in his teeth and leave him there." He smiles at me in an irritatingly smug way.

"We don't need him anyway, Stiletto. You and I can handle this show on our own. Let's get over to Koots before he cries to Maestro. He's a tattletale. That's why we call him Rat," he says.

When we pull into the parking lot of Chilkoot Charlie's bar and lounge, Rat is standing outside with a small group of bikers, smoking a cigarette. He looks like he is irritated already. He waves for Dragonfly to lower his window so they can speak.

Rat starts yelling, "Fly, if you ever embarrass me in front of my lady friends again, you and I are going to have a big problem. I don't appreciate you disrespecting me like that."

Fly retorts, "You scumbag. I should jump from this car and punch you out right here, you lowlife puke. Stand down, Rat. I demand it."

Wow, the boys are going at it hot and heavy. We are starting to cause a scene in front of the bar, so I intervene. "Hey, listen up!" I yell.

Both of them go silent and dart me angry looks. "Dragonfly and I need to split. Back away from the car, Rat, before we all get into trouble with Maestro," I shout.

"Come on, let's go. Stomp on the gas pedal and get us out of here," I yell to Dragonfly.

Our car lurches from the parking lot out on to Spenard Road, going about 40 miles per hour. The smoke from our tires leaves a trail behind us, an eighth of a mile long, hanging in the cold air. As we drive over to Old Harbor Avenue, Dragonfly explains what we are doing.

"Stiletto, we have some high-value wildlife mounts packed inside the trunk in protective cases. View this transaction as an exchange of revenue. Something for something," Fly says. "This guy we are delivering to is making Maestro big money. We need to keep him happy. He has a morbid fascination with death and trophy wildlife mounts. So that's what we will bring him. He can have all the heads in Anchorage if he wants them," he explains. "Maestro is paying him with all of his African wildlife mounts and furs. He is also getting a bear rug wall mount. It is a diminutive bear species from outside of Alaska." "I've seen that bear rug wall mount. Did Maestro give him the shield and spear hanging on the wall by the big fireplace?" I ask Fly.

"No. He'll never give them up. Those were Maestro's words, not mine," he replies.

When we get to the house on Old Harbor Avenue, the driveway is empty, and it looks like no one is home. Dragonfly tells me not to worry about it as he backs our car into the driveway.

"We instructed him to leave the garage open for us. We need to lock it up for him after we unload the heads," Fly explains.

We get the large trunk of the car open. Everything is in cases or wrapped in blankets. The garage door is unlocked as Dragonfly said it would be. There is a small workshop area near the back wall where we place the wildlife mounts.

The house and surrounding yard seem orderly. The garage is clean and neat but cluttered.

"Are we going to be able to get everything in here?" I ask Dragonfly.

"Stack it up. We'll get it in, believe me, Stiletto. I am not leaving from here with any of this in my car. This guy owns it all now. He can do what he wants with it," he replies.

"Fly, I grew up hunting, and I have never understood having a dead animal staring at you? I realize to each their own, but when I am trying to relax and enjoy life, I would rather not be thinking about death," I reply.

"Exactly. I agree. Leave these filthy beasts in the woods where they belong. Eat them, for sure. Marvel at their beauty when they are alive. Just leave the heads in the grave with the rest of the waste from the kill," Dragonfly replies.

Chapter Sixteen

Lieutenant McCrackin Handles De Luciano's Concerns

Lieutenant McCrackin is speaking. "Specialist De Luciano, I am your main contact here in this unit. I have an open-door policy. You can counsel with me at any time of day or night. Is that understood, soldier?"

"Yes, sir, open-door policy. You made that clear several months ago. That's why I am here. We need to speak. I have a pressing concern," I reply.

"Okay, let me hear your concerns, Stiletto. What do you have for me?" he asks.

"To be clear, what I am about to say is disturbing to think about, Lieutenant," I reply.

Lieutenant McCrackin has a curious look on his face. He is leaning back in his chair, with his fingers steepled and his chin resting on his fingertips. "Continue. Please speak clearly," he says.

"This potential asset of ours down at 417 D Street has asked me to engage in some extremely unpleasant behavior. It has dire consequences for the intended victims of the crime," I reply.

"Go on, keep speaking," he says.

"Families are going to be torn with anguish. I mean, these guys are repulsive," I reply.

Lieutenant McCrackin is succinct with his request. "Give me straight talk, De Luciano. Don't hold back. In the end, you will not be responsible for their actions, soldier."

"Sir, I have been propositioned to join a kidnapping crew that is supplying human flesh to overseas buyers in South Africa. They want me to engage in snatch-and-grab kidnappings around the city of Anchorage. I would be tearing babies and young girls from their families," I explain.

His face turns very pale with shock. Slowly calculating his words before he speaks, he replies, "De Luciano, you need to stand down immediately. I will contact CID and run this up through our chain of command. Do not contact these individuals again unless I have instructed you to."

"Sir, if I break contact now, they will know for sure that I have not been all the way in with them. I need to continue my interactions, or I will be compromised. Once I'm compromised, we can't go back in there. None of us will get back in," I implore him.

The lieutenant knows I will keep insisting that the mission continues, so he gives in.

"Okay. You will need to stay vigilant, De Luciano. Stand strong, and stay in the game for us out there. If I receive orders to pull you back, you'll be the first person to know about it. It will be imperative that you react quickly and extract yourself from the situation."

Chapter Seventeen

La Metafora è un Capitano

(Translation from Italian to English: The metaphor is one captain.)

The building at 417 D Street, Anchorage, Alaska, is the headquarters of an organized crime organization. One of the businesses is Snoopy's Video Arcade and Tee-Shirt Shop, where Maestro usually meets his main guys. It's their hangout and has now become an intended kill zone.

Because the business is in a high activity zone, timing will be essential to limit our collateral damage. We have three targets in our sights. If we can kill them all at once, we can accomplish a coup de grace.

It's time for us to bring some violence of action to the streets of Anchorage and firepower for effect. We will need to exercise stealth for the mission to be a success.

The first target on our list is Maestro himself. The leader of an organized crime faction. He is directing a human trafficking ring out of Anchorage, Alaska, and committing other heinous crimes against the local community.

He also owns exotic dance clubs, a chain of liquor stores named Brown Jug, and a taxi cab company called Orange Taxi. All of them are booming and thriving cash businesses.

Next on our hit list is a ruthless street thug named Dragonfly. Dragonfly is the nastiest lieutenant on these streets. He patrols around Anchorage day and night in an Orange Taxi cab. Just muttering Dragonfly's name spreads fear into the recipient. If someone gets found swimming with the fish out in Cook Inlet, Dragonfly most likely puts them in that position.

The third target is a guy everyone knows as Rat. Rat is the proprietor at Snoopy's Video Arcade. All drugs and illicit contraband sold out of the store must go through Rat. He is also the adviser to the crime boss whose job is to assist guests, Maestro's guy who sets up all the meetings.

Fifteen dead or missing would be a slow quarter for these guys. They take their business seriously. To kill them all at once, someone needs to bring perfection from every direction. No hiccups, no wrinkles, or we all get sent to prison for the rest of our lives for illegal kills on civilians.

"I can get the explosives into the video arcade. Someone else will need to get into the adult bookstore next door. That's an easy mission. Walk in and go through the curtain into the back area where all the private booths are. I can get you the master key that opens all the money boxes. Select a booth to locate each explosive charge and place them inside the money boxes. Make sure your timers get set properly," I am explaining to my fire team.

"I'll tell Rat I can work next Saturday. That will give me ten hours to place and prime the explosives in that store. We go electrical detonation on this one. Two five-pound charges in each location individually primed and timed," I say.

"Roger that, Stiletto. I'll take the adult bookstore. I need to build my library. My mother keeps encouraging me to read more," Specialist Masters says with a teasing smile.

Sergeant Foche barks, "Listen up, this is serious business. Tone it down and follow Stiletto's directive without interjecting your sick street humor."

I respond, "Sarge makes a great point. We will be on our first military operation in urban terrain, using live explosives with intended targets. We don't want anything unintended to happen. Let's tighten it up and get real on this one."

A booming knock on the briefing chamber's door brings us all to attention. We watch as Sergeant Foche gets up to open the door and let the visitors inside.

"How can I help you, gentlemen?" Sergeant Foche asks.

"Sergeant, please step aside and allow us access to this briefing room. That's coming directly from General Masanotti," a loud voice declares from behind the door.

Two CID investigators walk into our meeting with an air of superiority about them. I recognize one of them as CID investigator Ringo Covert. The other one is a rookie I have never seen.

"Gentlemen of the first squad second platoon, listen up. To allow you tactical command of a downtown area, we will need to create a diversion. It would have to be major to be effective. We cannot allow it at this time," Covert explains.

"Alaska, in general, is in a period of unprecedented growth. Strictly from a financial perspective, the United States cannot, and will not, sanction this mission," he says.

He continues, "We have our people in place. They have eyes on the horizon. Some of those tenets are present with us here in this room today. Stay the course and stand down."

"Sir, with respect, these guys need to be stopped as soon as possible. We can't let this insidious behavior continue to terrorize this community," Sergeant Foche says.

"Sergeant Foche, we understand your position, and we sympathize with you, but you have received your orders. Now stand your guys down at this time," Investigator Covert says.

"Gentlemen, I need you all to listen up. Sometimes we are involved in things that are much bigger than ourselves. Right now is one of those times. I need you to exercise big-picture thinking for me. National security is imperative," he says.

I raise my hand and ask, "Investigator Covert, am I to carry on and proceed as directed?"

Covert seems greatly disgruntled and replies, "I have no idea what you are talking about, soldier. Have we ever met? Why are you addressing me like we know each other? Do I look like your friend, De Luciano? Stand down, scumbag. That's a direct order," he says. Both CID officers abruptly turn and storm out of the briefing room, slamming the door behind them.

Silence envelopes the room like a thick fog. Everyone is looking at each other with a look of defeat. Specialist Masters speaks first.

"I guess there will be no new reading material for me to ponder. There goes that plan right out the door," he says with his mischievous smile.

Ignoring Masters's comment, Sergeant Foche asks, "Stiletto, do you know of any fallback locations where we may be able to make contact with these guys?"

Cautiously, I respond, "I have heard them speaking of an area among the dangerously high rugged cliffs above Far North Bicentennial Park. They gather in front of a very steep rock face. I have heard them refer to it as the Precipice."

"You said you have never been up in there. Is this correct?" Foche asks.

"Yes, that is correct. I only venture into the mountains and above tree line with this team right here, Sergeant," I say.

"So the precipice is above tree line?" he asks.

"From what I have been told, yes. We will need to gain access from over near Cambell Airstrip Road. Do you want me to recon the area for an immersion point?" I ask.

"Let's do it. Will you need to take anyone with you, or can you go alone?" Foche asks.

"I am thinking if you send me with two guys, we will do an actual road recon so it will look like we are out there working. I will have PFC Townsend put on the team with his surveying equipment. Once we get all of our survey equipment set up, I can start taking pictures," I reply.

Sergeant Foche sits back and says, "Let's do this, gentlemen. I will run this up the flagpole with our immediate chain of command. No one will ever utter a word about this mission. If we target and kill civilians, it needs to stay within the room."

"Is this understood, first squad?" he barks.

"Yes, Sergeant. It stays in the room," we respond.

"First squad is second to none. We're the best. Forget the rest. Oorah!" the team replies.

Chapter Eighteen

Guys Gone Missing From E.4th Avenue and Ingra Street

Amidst a recent rise in missing person reports, the law enforcement community of Anchorage, Alaska, is on high alert. An Anchorage Police Department lieutenant named Maureen Dowd explains the complexities of serial murder to her team.

"The majority of the missing male prostitutes were last seen around the location of E.4th Avenue and Ingra Street. At this time, we have nine males reported missing. We do suspect foul play," Lieutenant Dowd tells her team.

"Are there any questions at this time?" she asks.

"I have a question, Lieutenant. I am curious if we are thinking there may be a connection to the rising number of missing female prostitutes and exotic dancers from that same area?" Corporal Williams asks.

"Good question, Corporal. If not, maybe we need to be. A number of those women went missing less than a half-mile away from E.4th Avenue and Denali Street.

DIAMONDS IN THE ROUGH, WITHERING DISAPPROVAL

We may have located one of the killer's anchor points," Lieutenant Dowd responds.

Meanwhile, out on the lonely streets, Stiletto is patrolling E.4th Avenue and finds himself down at the corner of E.4th Avenue and Ingra Street. It's cold, and there's a stiff wind blowing down out of the frontal range of the looming Chugach Mountains.

Why is this truck slowing down? Who is this guy looking at me? The wide-eyed driver is nodding his head toward me, indicating he wants to pull over and speak with me.

Hold on for a second. I've seen this guy cruising the girls over near A Street. After flicking my cigarette at his truck, I pick up an empty beer can and throw it toward him. I tear into him with a verbal tirade and start chasing him down the street.

The truck speeds away from me in a cloud of dust. A bright blue Cadillac pulls up next to me, beeping its horn. A bearded man leans out the front passenger window and screams, "Hey, good-looking!"

I ignore the Cadillac. Walking over to two guys standing on the nearby corner, I ask them, "Have you guys been standing out here on this corner for a long time?"

They glance at each other, and one of them asks me, "Are you a cop or something, man?"

"No. I am not a cop. Why? Do I look like a cop to you?" I ask.

"You do kind of look like a cop. If you're not the police, then why were you chasing that truck?" he asks.

"The guy driving the truck is a known troublemaker. Do you know anyone who has gone with him? Have any of your friends jumped into his truck?" I ask.

He replies, "No, man. Calm down. We just got into Anchorage and don't know much of anyone yet. We are hoping to find a party tonight, so we can try to meet some people."

"Be careful when you are walking around out here. People call me Stiletto on the streets in town. If anyone gives you a hard time, let me know," I say.

"Nice to meet you, Stiletto. I'm Nick. My friend is Tony. Hopefully, we can avoid trouble," Nick says.

"Nice to meet you, Tony. My name is Anthony also, but no Tony, please. Never call me Tony, and we can stay friends," I tease.

Both guys laugh and shout, "Hey, Stiletto, if you are ever looking for a good time, look us up. We can take care of you. You would be in good hands."

"Yeah, right. Thanks for the offer, but that's never happening. You boys keep safe out here," I reply.

These guys need to realize that dire circumstances can befall the unwary on these cold, windy streets. The rules are to keep your head up and your nose into the wind out here. Always be careful, watch for possible danger or difficulties at all times. Take a step back at every corner before crossing the street and stay vigilant.

Chapter Nineteen

A Dusty Parking Lot Murder full of Shame

A tsunami of shame rages in his mind, roiling, seething, feeding his homicidal frenzy. The maniac has become unleashed and knows no boundaries. He seems to be uncontrolled and roaming the streets free.

What's wrong with me? What have I become? It's one thing to kidnap a woman, but a guy? It's only oral sex. Right? the monster reasons within his faltering mind.

"I know a nice place where we can park down by the water. We will be there in a couple of minutes," I say. The kid nods his approval but keeps staring out the passenger window as we drive down to the waterfront.

"How long have you been up here in Alaska. Are you just visiting, or do you plan on staying here to live?" I ask him.

His answer is vague. "Not long. Maybe like four months tops," he replies.

"Do you like it up here so far?" I pry.

"Not really. Can we get to where we are going already?" he asks.

"S . . . sure. No problem," I respond.

"What's your name. What should I call you while we do it?" I ask.

"You can call me Nick. Nick's my name," he says.

As soon as I get my truck parked in a far corner of the parking lot, I backfist Nick in his face. When his hands go up to protect himself, I grab his left wrist and wrap a handcuff around it. As we struggle, he spits at me and starts screaming, "Stop this. What are you trying to do to me? Stop this right now."

"Calm down, Nick," I shout at him. "If you do what I tell you, everything will go well for you tonight. Now shut up and calm down over there," I say.

Nick's eyes are bulging as he pulls against his restraint; red-faced, he snarls, "I hate you. Stop this right now. Why are you doing this to me? Are you the guy that's killing everyone? Are you the guy?"

Pointing my gun at his head, I say, "This will all be over quick if you calm down. Now stop your crying, and let's do what you do," I demand.

I've always loved this drive through the golf course up into Arctic Valley. You go over the hill and around the bend into the sunset. As I am loading Nick's dead body onto my transport wagon, I am thankful I changed the original tires for these blue balloon aftermarket tires. The wide wheels travel across the muddy trail much better.

Chapter Twenty

What's that Black Confetti in the Sky?

Swirling beacons of the afterlife. The symbolic meaning of the raven in Native American Indian culture describes the bird as a creature of metamorphosis. It symbolizes change and transformation, a shift from one reality to another.

Ravens announce messages from deep within the void of the cosmos. They bring knowledge from beyond space and time, nestled within their midnight wings. They approach those within the tribe who the cosmos deems worthy of receiving the messages.

The first squad of the second platoon, 562nd Engineer Company, is nestled among the devil's club growing on the banking above the Doyon Utility powerline. Devil's club is part of the underlying layer of vegetation in the rainforests of the Pacific Northwest, noted for its woody stems covered in irritating thorns. It causes red rashes and extremely itchy skin.

Sergeant Blankenship is addressing his squad. "Someone's involved in some killing down there. In the killing fields of Vietnam, the ravens always gathered after every battle, but I have never seen this many birds in one location," he says.

PFC Daniels speaks up. "It looks like black confetti is swirling on the horizon. I've never seen anything like this. I agree with Sarge; something nasty is happening down there."

"You're all crazy. It's just a moose hunter burying their carcass. In Alaska, people kill things and bury the remains all the time," Private Nelson replies.

Blankenship retorts, "I'll repeat myself. Human remains are down there. That's a fact I strongly believe based on my experience. Have you ever done any killing, Nelson?"

Specialist Conlon speaks, "I vote for a recon team to go down. Let's send fire team A down to scout around for forty-five minutes," he suggests.

Sergeant Blankenship disagrees with him. "No. We already sent the team down. They recorded what they observed, and we escalated it through proper channels. Now we will wait for their response," he says.

"Is local law enforcement being made aware of what we are hearing and seeing? Are they going to ignore this and allow it to continue?" Specialist Conlon asks in disbelief.

"Gentlemen, I am just as concerned as every person in this group is about this. We have done our jobs for now. I suggest we back off and allow local law enforcement to pursue this at their own pace," Sergeant Blankenship advises us.

He continues, "Our job is not to investigate ongoing criminal activity. We get sent into the field to observe and record real-time data. We then follow good practice by disseminating that information across our chain of command. That's it."

Chapter Twenty-One

The FBI Briefs AST on De Luciano

"Ladies and gentlemen, let's bring this meeting to order, please," FBI Agent Pomicter requests.

He yells out, "Recording the date and time. Today's date is December 3, 2020. The time is 0400 hours. Our location is the FBI field office located in Anchorage, Alaska."

Agent Pomicter continues, "I am FBI agent James Pomicter. Present in the room with me are FBI agent Veronica Sage, Alaska State Trooper Cold Case investigator Randall McPherson, and Alaska State Trooper Cold Case investigator Wendy Simeon."

"Thank you for coming here today for this debriefing," Pomicter says while he removes a cover that is protecting an erasable board hanging on the wall in front of him.

"In April 2020, Investigator McPherson was alerted by AST Commander Merrill of an impending phone call about serial killer Damon Dirks. The phone call was coming from a person claiming to have pertinent information regarding the location of a large burial site that may be associated with Damon Dirk's missing homicide victims."

Pomicter continues, "The caller also claims to have witnessed a number of these homicides from the surrounding ridgelines above the Doyon Utility powerline in Arctic Valley while on duty with the US Army back in 1981, 1982, and 1983."

"Am I on point so far with my information, Randall?" Pomicter asks McPherson.

"Yes, sir. Spot on," Officer McPherson says.

Pomicter continues, "This individual was a known entity to us back in the day. As you can see here on this big board, he is listed with Damon Dirks as an individual of concern, moving and operating within the adult entertainment industry. We never suspected De Luciano of committing any of the killings. He was a force to be considered. Violence followed him everywhere he went," Pomicter explains. "We know he was unleashed on the streets by this guy here, Maestro. De Luciano protected most of Maestro's businesses. More importantly, De Luciano's fighting skills kept him close to the red light district of Anchorage. Close to the women."

"Agent Sage will take the briefing over from here. She has more insight on De Luciano to share with us," Agent Pomicter announces.

A stunning presence in any room, Veronica Sage approaches the picture board with the utmost confidence in her steps. She is poised as she takes the podium.

"We now believe De Luciano was a recruiter for Maestro. He would find exotic dancers that wanted to join the fraternity. This fraternity I am referring to was a group of spiritual magicians. That's how they referred to themselves—spiritual magicians," she says.

"De Luciano would find women to play the roles of enchantress and priestess. An enchantress acts as a head priestess. The criteria was straightforward. Dark hair, younger than twenty-five years old, no tattoos and any ethnicity," Sage explains. "I have met Anthony De Luciano. One of his many skills is making people feel wanted and excepted. He is likable and good at what he does. When I worked with Anthony, I felt at times like I was hanging out with my little brother. He's that good at what he does," she says.

"Anthony has credibility. He was there and interacted with these people. They shared with him a lot of inside information. He had eyes on Dirks in multiple settings, but it does not mean he was a coconspirator to murder," Agent Sage explains.

Agent Pomicter raises his hand and speaks. "I believe he came forward to do the right thing. Now he is being implicated by circumstantial evidence. In today's world, we have a lot of eyes on us. Let's tread carefully on this one. The last thing we would want is to ruin the life of an individual trying to work with law enforcement. Mr. De Luciano has been open and available to cooperate with us. He helped us connect Damon Dirks to the kidnappings in midtown. By doing this, he has made himself a potential target of revenge. We might not agree with what he stood for back then, and we do not agree with how he disseminated his information through his books, but we should respect the fact that he did come forward," Agent Pomicter concludes.

Chapter Twenty-Two
An Accusation is not a Charge

"Mr. De Luciano, I am expensive. For me to defend you on this type of charge, my fees would have to begin at thirty thousand dollars just to get started," attorney Harrington explains to me. I can initiate contact with law enforcement for twenty-five hundred dollars using a letter of inquiry into the status of any forthcoming charges they may have against you. Is this something you want me to do for you at this time?" he asks.

Wow, thirty thousand dollars. Why did I become involved in all of this? What made me step forward? How did I find myself sinking in the deep end of the swimming pool?

"No. Not at this time, Mr. Harrington. I firmly believe, sometimes the best thing to do is nothing at all and wait it out," I reply.

"Remember this, Mr. De Luciano, an accusation is not a charge. A charge is not a conviction. To connect and charge you with circumstantial evidence, the existing evidence against you would need to be substantive," Harrington explains.

"Anthony, if law enforcement made the request, would you be willing to be interrogated while connected to a truth analysis system?" he asks me.

"I don't see why not. Sure thing. If I need to, let's do it," I reply.

In the meantime, sitting in a dimly lit office over at 5700 East Tudor Road, Alaska state trooper Randy McPherson is agitated by his thoughts. His assistant AST officer, Wendy Simeon, listens as he speaks.

"Wendy, am I wrong with my assessment? Alaska state troopers have been waiting for thirty-eight years to get their hands on this information. Damon Dirks has been a dark stain on law enforcement history in Alaska. This new information could enlarge that stain if not handled properly," he says.

"We have always had, and still have, jurisdiction up in Arctic Valley. Now, FBI National Affairs is stepping in to take over. I find it frustrating that they can push us out of the way on this one," he continues.

"This is our worst-case scenario. A former soldier discharged under honorable conditions who knowingly moved illicit product through Alaskan military bases unabated. There was no stopping or slowing this guy down back in the day," McPherson sneers. "This guy, De Luciano, was a known entity back then. CID was all over him. FBI was and is still tracking him. Now, thirty-eight years later, he leads us to a massive graveyard on the outskirts of the municipality, right on the edge of Fort Richardson. This guy has some credibility," McPherson states. Seemingly perplexed by the context of the ongoing dialogue, Officer Simeon inquires, "Are we going to allow this outsider to come into Alaska after all this time and profit from his knowledge? Are we going to allow him to become the next expert on Damon Dirks?"

Randy McPherson retorts, "Not if I have anything to do with it. Not on my watch."

"That is my train of thought also, sir. We can't let him win. If the public is led to believe De Luciano solved this on his own, his credibility will skyrocket," Simeon says.

Officer McPherson leans back in his chair and shakes his head with an air of disbelief.

"Any news stream that De Luciano is associated with will put him in a position to profit. He may have us locked in a stalemate situation. We need to dissolve his integrity, shatter his image," he says with a condescending sneer.

Chapter Twenty-Three

Maestro's Killing Adventure on African Safari

Africa. Voodoo adherents. Wealthy international elite. Maestro puts his question to me like this. "Stiletto, imagine with me for a moment being able to hunt another human being just for fun. Can you picture this?"

"You seem to forget my job in the military. I train to hunt human beings all of the time. I imagine it every night before I fall asleep. Whether I want to do it or not is another question," I reply.

"This is different. I am talking about being able to choose your victim. Set up the kill zone the way you want it. Adorn it with artifacts and all that glitters. How does this sound to you?" he asks.

"Well, again, that's an integral part of my job. Identify the targets, then lure them into a kill zone prepared for the ambush. Sometimes, we do stage the kill site with tools and debris," I retort.

"No need to get hostile with me. I fully realize you are one of Uncle Sam's elite. I've seen you in action," he smirks.

"Listen, Stiletto. I am talking about buying a fantasy, having the money and the privilege to hunt another human being because you can afford to. Recreational killing because you want to. Exercising free will—it's a choice that you make," Maestro explains.

"Maestro, the day I graduated basic training from Fort Leonard Wood, a senior drill instructor who had spent three tours fighting in Vietnam proclaimed from the stage during our graduation commencement, 'Gentlemen, you are now licensed by Uncle Sam to hunt and kill another human being legally for your country,'" I explain to him.

"Would you forget about Vietnam? I am talking big game hunting in South Africa, man. Human beings for thrills. Vietnam. Get off the Nam tour and join me in Africa someday, Stiletto," he implores.

Removing his sunglasses, he demands, "Look at me. Look into my eyes, Stiletto."

With a snarl, he fervently asks me, "Do I look like a monkey to you, Stiletto? Do I look like a monkey to you? I've climbed to the top of the food chain along with my ancestors. I kill and eat whatever I want, whenever I want. Do you understand me?"

"Honestly, I don't understand you, Maestro. I want to forget what you are talking about and have a good time tonight. Is that too much to ask?" I reply.

He detonates with rage, as I have never experienced from another human being before. Ashen-faced and snarling like a vicious wolf, he rants.

"You don't understand me? Who cares what you understand? Do you think I brought you into my home tonight to get your approval? Do you, Stiletto? Answer me, you little puke, right now," he demands.

"Maestro, my invitation said cocktail gathering. I came here to party, not fight. I came to unwind, not think about death and killing," I retort.

Enraged, he lashes out and slaps me across my face. Before my head finishes spinning, he drops to one knee and punches me in my stomach. The power of the punch knocks the wind out of me. I stumble back against the fireplace and trip on the corner of the hearth.

Maestro starts running toward me like a raging bull screaming, "Thunder!"

Rat comes running in from another room. Screaming at me, he gets in between Maestro and myself. "Stiletto, stop. Don't do anything. Stop this right now."

Before I can reply, Rat yells, "If you make your move, I will have to kill you right here."

Chapter Twenty-Four

Maestro Questions Stiletto's Family Ties

"Take a ride with me, Stiletto. We need to go talk about something right now," Maestro says.

"Sure thing, boss. Let's go," I reply. We leave the store, walk outside, and get into a black Ford Mustang with two white racing stripes painted on the hood. Maestro drives us.

"This thing is a beast. How long have you owned this baby?" I ask him as we turn left on to W. 4th Avenue. He glances over at me but doesn't answer my question. He is clenching the steering wheel and humming a tune lightly under his breath as he drives.

"Stiletto, you are like the son I have never had. If I did have a son, I would want him to be just like you. Do you come from a big family?" he asks.

Huh? Why is he asking me about my family? Maestro has never asked about my family. Why now? Is he planning something against me? Am I going to be killed?

"Yes, a big Italian family that cares about me. Why do you ask?" I inquire.

"Curious, that's all; no need to be concerned. I am trying to learn a little more about you. When do you discharge out of the Army?" he asks.

"I have one more year left on my contract. I'm cycling out of Alaska soon. Right now, my next duty station has yet to be determined. Why do you want to know that?" I ask.

"As I said before, my curiosity is at a high level right now. I am sniffing around, trying to get my house in order. Straighten up some loose ends," he retorts.

Here it is. I'm a dead man. "Loose ends? Now I'm loose ends? Are you kidding me, Maestro?" I ask.

"No. No, you have it all wrong, Stiletto. You are going to help me tie up some loose ends. You're going with me to Hawaii in September. All expenses paid for three weeks. How does that sound?" he asks.

"Hawaii? Why are we going to Hawaii?" I ask.

"I have multiple ventures based in Hawaii. I just got a piece of a small airport over there, and I need you and Dragonfly to do some errands for me. It will take several weeks, but you two will have plenty of time for relaxation," he says.

"Maestro, why me? Why do you think I am one of your guys for this job?" I ask.

"Stiletto, I have explained this to you before. No one can get to you with material circumstances or cash gifts," he replies.

"Why would I want all that glitters? I don't need jewelry. I don't need cars. I'm not into fancy and elegant women," I say.

"See what I mean? Did you listen to yourself?" he asks me.

"You keep telling me I am the son you never had. That makes you my stepfather. You always tell me cash is king. My goal is cash. Cash that I earn. I want to own multiple businesses as you do. Cash businesses," I reply.

"If I do this thing you're asking me to do over in Hawaii, how much does it pay?" I ask him.

"How much does it pay? I just told you all expenses will be paid, didn't I? Are you saying you are expecting compensation beyond that?" he asks me.

"Of course, why wouldn't I? You keep telling me to demand what I am worth out there," I reply.

"Let me hear what you think you are worth on this one, Stiletto? Go ahead and tell me what you want to get paid. Let me hear the number for three weeks?" Maestro asks.

"I need to get paid thirty-nine thousand three hundred dollars per week," I reply.

"That's a pretty exact number you just quoted me. Do you have a plan for the money?" he asks.

"Yes. I am looking at a large tract of land south of Rabbit Creek Road. It's approximately 354 acres of buildable land. There's a gravel road already cut in that divides the middle of the property," I explain.

"Well, let me think about it. I can certainly afford to pay you that number. If I ask you to bring some violence of action to the streets of Honolulu, would you be willing?" he asks.

"Of course. I'll start training now. I'm working out with the brigade boxing champion. I am helping the team get ready for the next fight. Lawrence Travers from Shreveport, Louisiana. They call him Mr. T. on base. He fought down at Gussie Lamours in the first televised Mr. Alaskan tough guy competition. I was his ring manager for that fight. We know Alaska's heavyweight boxing champion, J.J. Jackson."

I guarantee him I will be ready for the violence. Like a friend, we will call upon the growling beast from deep within. Eyes bulging, clenched fists lashing, bones will disintegrate into gristle under the withering sun of Honolulu.

Chapter Twenty-Five:

The Mind of a Bereaved Father

"Dr. Morgan, lately, I seem to be unraveling. I can't think straight. Am I beyond repair"? I ask my psychiatrist.

"No. This level of grief is normal at this stage of the recovery process," Dr. Morgan informs me. She continues with her observations.

"When a father loses his daughter, as you have Tom, the feelings of despair can be overwhelming. For some time, your feelings are going to be disproportionately excessive," she says.

"That's an understatement. My biggest anguish is that I couldn't protect my daughter when she needed me the most. I can hear her screaming in my mind. When will it go away? How did we fail her?" I respond.

"Tom, I would like to encourage you not to concentrate on what you may have done wrong," she says.

"Then what should I be concentrating on?" I interrupt her.

"I really can't tell you what to do at this point, Tom," she replies.

"This is infuriating me, Dr. Morgan. You encourage me not to take a course of action, but when I ask you what I should be doing, you can't tell me? Enough of this foolishness already. Thank you for your time, Doctor," I retort.

"Tom, please slow down. Don't self-destruct right now," she implores.

Dr. Morgan continues, "You are your number one top priority. Your physical and mental well-being is of the utmost importance at this moment. That's your focus."

After taking several deep breaths, I explain, "Listen, doc, you seem like a genuine person who truly cares. I feel like a gunpowder keg, heated, ready to ignite and detonate. I wouldn't want to hurt you in any way."

"Tom, I appreciate you being so candid and vulnerable. It's a part of my job to absorb a certain level of brutality from my clients. You are doing fine. Keep going," she prods.

Does this lady understand I want to kill everyone I see? Snuff out all the people that stand before me. Let me try to make this clear without scaring her.

"Dr. Morgan, I am going to use your first name for emphasis. I do not mean to disrespect you in any way. I am stressed with regards to my mindset," I say.

Deciding not to wait for her to respond, I continue, "Now listen closely, Judy. I am so close to the edge, I almost killed an older man coming here today because he waved to me. He waved hello, and I wanted to murder him. Do you understand this?" I ask.

Dr. Morgan gathers herself and responds, "Tom, this is also normal. You are moving through the stages of grief at a very healthy pace."

"Stages of grief. Stages of grief?" I remark mockingly.

"Have you ever lost a child to a sadistic killer, Doctor?" I demand of her.

"Tom, I surely do not know what you are going through. I have no way of knowing what you feel. I am not trying to tell you how to feel. I am trying to guide and help you establish a process to grieve. That's my job. That's it," she explains.

"I'm dealing with my wife's grief also, Dr. Morgan. How do I cope with her? She has crawled up inside of herself. Donna had our baby ripped from her hands on a cold, thankless day in downtown Anchorage, Alaska. How do we deal with that, Doctor?" I plead with her. "I'm supposed to be strong for her, and I'm supposed to stay strong for the community at the same time?" I ask.

"Tom, you're not responsible for Donna's grief. She has to navigate that for herself. You must deal with your issues first. As far as the community goes, we are all behind you," she says.

"If only I had held Sandra more tightly the last time I saw her. Maybe if I had gone to the festival with my wife and baby, this wouldn't have happened? I hate myself, Doctor. If I could push a button and exterminate myself right now, I would do it," I say.

Chapter Twenty-Six

Officer McPherson Reveals a Killer's Hidden Mind

Bespectacled and sitting in a dimly lit corner of the room, Officer McPherson is shuffling a stack of photos from recent crime scenes. While taking a long gulp of his coffee, he looks up toward the other law enforcement officers in the room.

"I want to start our discussion with the logical steps we take when investigating homicide cases. We know most homicides get committed by someone known to the victim, so we focus on the relationships closest to the victim. It's a successful strategy for most of our murder investigations," he says.

Sighing, he continues, "Here's the tricky aspect of serial murder—the majority of serial murderers are not acquainted with or involved in a consensual relationship with their victims. It's more of an uncertain undertaking to investigate than other homicides. For the most part, serial murder involves strangers with no visible relationship between the offender and the victim. Lacking a connection between the offender and the victim, we need to attempt to identify the motivations behind the murders as a way to narrow our investigative focus," he explains.

"Human beings are complex creatures. Currently, four types of serial killers are on law enforcement's radar screen. These are visionary, mission-oriented, hedonistic, and last but not least, is the power and control killer," McPherson states.

Randy continues, "These types are identified based on their motivations for carrying out their crimes. For example, a hedonistic killer might kill for his sexual gratification. On the other hand, a visionary killer could murder people because he believes God is telling him to do so."

"As you can see, there are various reasons why serial killers kill. It becomes multifaceted and multilayered," he says. "Another point worth noting is that these motivations will often overlap. A killer can fall into more than one category. As I stated before, human beings are complex creatures. Therefore, we must be cautious about trying to organize every killer into one specific type or category."

He pauses and continues, "So what we have are four main types of serial killers that can be categorized as follows: A visionary killer believes that a person or entity is commanding them to kill. This type of killer most likely suffers some form of psychosis. They tend to lose touch with reality. Then we have mission-oriented killers. They kill to rid society of a certain group of people. Some of them see it as a cleansing mission. They take their job seriously.

Next up is the hedonistic killer. This person commits the acts for his pleasure. The usual reasons are going to be rape, torture, or money. In addition, the hedonistic killer often gets divided into three secondary categories labeled as lust, thrill, and comfort killers. Last on our list is the power and control freak. This animal fantasizes about having power. This person seeks to dominate and control their victims. Humiliation is an integral aspect of their acts," McPherson explains to the silent room.

"Are there any questions for me at this time?" he asks.

"Officer McPherson, what categories have we put our killer into, if any?" Officer Simeon asks.

"Good question, Wendy. That is what we are going to look at next. At this point, the FBI and Alaska State Trooper profilers have identified two or three categories our guy fits into," Randy explains. "Let us take a closer look and break them down now."

"We believe we have a mission-orientated serial killer on our hands, someone who kills to rid society of a specific group of people. In our case, he is targeting female sex workers and exotic dancers. We now believe he is also targeting male sex workers. This kind of killer believes that he is doing society a favor. In his head, he has a purpose. It is his mission to kill these people. As a result, he won't stop until he has been killed or caught by law enforcement. That's us." McPherson states.

"Listen closely. An important point to note is that this killer is not psychotic. Unlike the visionary killer, the mission-orientated killer is not out of touch with reality. He does not suffer from hallucinations or delusions. Some

God or other entity is not commanding him to commit these acts. His decision to kill is a decision that he makes all by himself. We also believe we have a hedonistic serial killer. This serial killer kills for pleasure. They are motivated by sex, the thrill of the kill, or money. Sometimes all three. A subcategory of the hedonistic killer is the lust killer. Does anyone want to guess what motivates a lust killer?" Randy asks.

Nobody decides to guess, so he continues to speak. "A lust killer is a serial killer who rapes, mutilates, and kills for his sexual gratification. In other words, the act of raping, torturing, and doing unspeakable things gives him intense feelings of pleasure. This violent fantasy will dominate their thoughts to the point that it becomes a deep-seated need. Once a lust killer commits his first murder, this part of him can take over his life. As time goes on, he might require more frequent stimulation to relive the highs of his first couple of kills. As he wrestles to control his urges and desire to act, the time between each murder may continue to get shorter and shorter. This kind of serial killer tends to use weapons that put them in close contact with their victim. For example, they may use a knife or strangle the victim with their hands."

"We believe there is a mission-orientated, hedonistic, lust killer on the prowl in our community at this time. This person has a big appetite for blood, and the beast is hungry," he concludes.

Chapter Twenty-Seven

Prolific Serial Killer Robert Hansen's Midnight Fires

Serial killer Robert Christian Hansen of Iowa became a volunteer fireman in 1960. That same year, he committed arson by igniting a school bus garage. He was arrested and sentenced to three years in prison. He only served twenty months of his sentence. It was revenge arson.

"What's the difference between an arsonist and a pyromaniac?" Agent Sage asks the room.

"Pyromania is a psychiatric condition that deals with impulse control. Arson is a criminal act. It's usually done maliciously and with criminal intent. Both are intentional, but pyromania is most likely related to an irresistible urge within the person," Agent Pomicter replies.

Pomicter continues to explain, "Fire setting is an irresistible impulse for some, recognized as a form of mental illness. Fire becomes a weapon of vengeance used for some other secret, harmful, or destructive aim. Keep in mind, fire setting is not a clear-cut disorder, but behavior that stems from another deep-seated cause and effect."

"Excellent exchange of information, Agent Pomicter. Thank you. Can anyone tell us what the number one motive for arson is?" Veronica asks.

Investigator Simeon speaks up. "The most common motives for wildfire arson in Alaska include crime concealment. Fires are used for covering up a murder, burglary, or to eliminate evidence left at a crime scene," she says.

"That's correct, Officer Simeon, but crime concealment only appears to be related to three percent of wildfire arson cases in Alaska," Veronica explains. "Another motive we have identified across the broader spectrum is revenge arson. Fifty-three percent of wildfire cases in our state appear to be related to retaliation."

"Anthony De Luciano has repeatedly stated that they observed large bonfires burning during the homicides they listened in on. It seems these fires were controlled and possibly being used to create and alleviate fear simultaneously. Fear in the victim but a sense of well-being in Damon Dirks," Agent Sage speculates.

Officer Simeon speaks up and asks, "Agent Sage, where is the revenge motive in these fires witnessed up in Arctic Valley? De Luciano has also stated they did not ignite anything outside of the firepits."

"Good question, Wendy. The revenge is weaved in with the fear factor on a psychological level. He is scaring the women as an act of revenge. Filling them with fear is a large part of his retribution," Veronica says.

"How could the fires possibly bring fear to the women? We can speculate. You're a woman chained to a tree by Damon Dirks. You realize you are within the municipality near an occupied building. You can see the lights from that building. Hope starts to build. Maybe someone will see the smoke or the light from the fire. According to De Luciano, most of the time, these fires would start between eight and nine o'clock in the evening, accompanied by screaming and shouting for help. As time goes on, your hope of being rescued starts to fade. Despair sets in until you become despondent when you realize this guy is not afraid of being detected. Your tormentor's antics escalate into the evening. De Luciano reported the murders would happen at midnight preceded by a higher frequency of attacks just before Dirks finished with them."

"Remember, everyone. There is a routine. It is complex and multilayered. All of it designed to intimidate and petrify the victims before and while he kills them," she concludes.

Chapter Twenty-Eight

If Serial Killer Robert Hansen had Freely Lived on

Imagine for a moment if the beast had been allowed to evolve. What's in a person's mind that kills for fun? How could any of us know unless we have also murdered on a recreational basis?

He got lost living amongst their screams and stench, dancing in front of the flames before he terminated their existence. Incorrigible and naughty is what he accused them of being, heaping withering disapproval upon their slumped shoulders.

I love my daughter, but I feel like strangling her once in a while. I can't shake this nagging thought from my mind. *Could I kill my daughter if I had to?*

"I can't allow this to happen, Dolly. I won't let people see you going around town with this John character. He is not good for you. I feel uneasy with that leather jacket he is always wearing. Does he own a motorcycle? And what's the story with the red bandana he has wrapped around his forehead all the time, about. Is he part of a criminal gang?" I ask my daughter. Her arms folded tightly, she has a look of bewilderment as she replies, "Dad, please stop attacking him. John is not a bad guy. He treats me special and tells me how beautiful I am. He's never tried any funny business, so relax."

"R—relax? Did you tell me to relax, little girl?" I demand from her.

I don't wait for my daughter Dolly to respond. I continue to engage her verbally. "I'll relax when you stop being a bad girl and do as I ask. As long as you live under this roof and live in my house, it's my way or the Glenn Highway. It's your choice, little girl," I say.

Is she going to make me fly her out? How can I think these thoughts about my daughter? When did she become this despicable? Have we failed her as parents?

"Dolly, will you have time to come with me over to Merrill Field tomorrow?" I ask her.

Noticeably agitated with me, rolling her eyes with eyebrows raised, she responds, "Why?"

"I thought you might want to help me clean the airplane. Maybe afterward, we can go for a short flight up north to scout around?" I say.

"That's your thing. I'm not into flying, Dad. Plus, it's cold and windy up in the sky." My daughter is a drama queen, so she shivers for emphasis.

"Well, maybe we can do something else together then. I wouldn't want you to get cold. I have to go up into Arctic Valley to take down a tree stand I have set up along the powerline trail behind the Doyon Utility power plant. Maybe you can come with me and do that?" I implore.

Noticeably hesitant, she responds, "Sure. Yeah. Ok, if it will get you off of my back, I'll go with you tomorrow up into Arctic Valley for a hike along the powerline trail."

"Do me a favor. Please don't tell your mother or anyone else about our plans. Just in case we get back late, I don't want anyone worrying about us when we are up in there. There are a lot of bears walking around, and people get overly concerned," I say.

"One other thing I need to talk to you about, if we get stopped by the military when we are up in there tomorrow, let me do all of the talking. Can you do that for me, Dolly?" I ask.

She nods her approval and says, "Yeah, sure, no problem, Dad. It will be our secret. I'll never tell anyone I went in there with you if that's what you want me to do."

Chapter Twenty-Nine

Inception of Andrea's Dream

"Andrea, why would you want to do this? Are you sure about it? If I agree to introduce you to these guys, there may be no turning back. Let me make this clear. If they make you an offer to join their group to perform private shows and you say yes, there is no getting out for you. The Fraternity of Sisters is a dedicated core group of adherents. They also engage in private rituals that require dance. Is this the only reason you wanted to meet me last week? Is there any other reason you wanted to speak with me out here?" I ask her.

"No, Little Brother, it is not the only reason I wanted to meet you. I need protection, and I am finding myself attracted to you differently. I'm all confused right now. Please don't pressure me," Andrea responds.

"Follow me. We'll take a walk down by Cook Inlet. We can go over to Elderberry Park and sit there for a while," I reply.

DIAMONDS IN THE ROUGH, WITHERING DISAPPROVAL

We start walking in silence. As we approach the waterfront area, a gradually increasing sound becomes the lonely cries of a flock of seagulls. Andrea takes my hand.

"You know what I think would make the waterfront in Anchorage a lot better? A beach where we could swim in the inlet with the beluga whales. Would you swim with a pod of beluga if you could?" she asks me.

"Sounds idyllic. Instead of an inlet, we will call it a lagoon. White sand, white whales, snow-capped peaks, and suntanned humans for a little contrast," I reply.

Andrea laughs and hugs my arm while telling me about her family back in Hawaii.

"My father hates me, Little Brother. He is prominent in my home state. He despises my choices and has turned me into the black sheep of the whole family. Even my sister has turned her back on me. I don't know where to turn for help out here," she says.

"What makes you think you need help? Has someone threatened you? Are you in trouble out here?" I ask her.

"Not really. The guys that brought me to Alaska made a lot of promises. None of the promises came true. I want to forge my path now. Forget the lies and live my life," she says.

She continues to present her idea in detail. "I want to find my path to prosperity. I don't just want to live, I want to flourish. I want to live my life as a bright star," she says.

Andrea stands up and starts dancing. "Like a moth attracted to the light, I want to keep dancing beneath the moon. I want my show to continue after the curtains go down." She smiles.

"You have some big aspirations, sister. Now you will need to define what your actual dream is. Once you have a concept envisioned, never let it go. Keep it growing and dream on," I reply.

"Will you help me keep my dream alive, Little Brother? Promise me you will never let Andrea's dream die. I need you to promise me right now," she demands with a flirtatious smile.

I stand up and take her hand. I'm overwhelmed and don't know what to say. This girl has opened up to me in a big way. I feel emotionally vulnerable. Maybe even liable to higher penalties if I fail to protect her.

"Honestly, I just came out for a walk today. I didn't expect to meet you. Now here we are, getting involved on a personal level. The quickness of it is overwhelming me," I reply.

"This is simple. Do you want to be my friend?" she asks.

"Yes, I want to be your friend," I reply.

"I'm not preaching to you, but one of my favorite Bible quotes mentions no greater love has a man than this, that he lay down his life for his friends. Are you willing to lay your life down for me, Little Brother?" Andrea asks me.

"You're the boss. Yes, Andrea. I'm willing to lay my life down for you and keep your dream alive," I promise her.

Smiling, she gently pushes me backward, saying, "Good answer. Dream on, Little Brother. Dream on."

Epilogue

Time as a Filter

I've had forty years to process my grief, and I feel much more ready now to try and be a voice for change than I was back then. Time as a filter brings clarification.

When you write books such as I have, inspired by true, actual events with a backdrop story that includes torture and murder, the emotional turmoil is exhausting. It strains all of your relationships. Sometimes to the breaking point of no return.

Your life becomes the story, the whole story, and nothing but the story. It grips your soul and keeps pulling you back down like a torrent current. Can you hear that sucking sound all around you? It's your spirit trying to escape from the blistering torment.

When someone like Robert Hansen, a one-person killing machine, goes on a violent, homicidal spree, there are many untold victims. Think of the women first, the victims.

Family and friends get crushed. Siblings become the forgotten mourners. Those among the ranks of law enforcement suffer. The image and security of the local community get shattered. Apprehension and tension rule the day.

Let us grieve with all of the families one last time. Please commend law enforcement for their tenacity over the years. Most importantly, be thankful for the life you live today.

Namaste.

www.ingramcontent.com/pod-product-compliance
Lightning Source LLC
Chambersburg PA
CBHW060844050426
42453CB00008B/826